EXPANDED EDITION
Grade 2

T0155157

The *If You Find a Rock* lesson is part of the Picture-Perfect STEM program K–2 written by the program authors and includes lessons from their award-winning series.

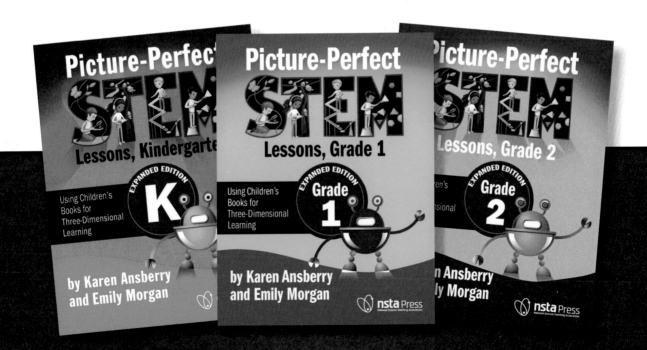

Picture-Perfect STEM Lessons, Kindergarten
Using Children's Books for Three-Dimensional Learning
EXPANDED EDITION K
by Karen Ansberry and Emily Morgan

Picture-Perfect STEM Lessons, Grade 1
Using Children's Books for Three-Dimensional Learning
EXPANDED EDITION Grade 1
by Karen Ansberry and Emily Morgan
nsta Press National Science Teaching Association

Picture-Perfect STEM Lessons, Grade 2
Using Children's Books for Three-Dimensional Learning
EXPANDED EDITION Grade 2
n Ansberry ly Morgan
nsta Press National Science Teaching Association

Additional information about using the Picture Perfect Science series, including key reading strategies, NGSS connections, and the BSCS 5E instructional model can be downloaded for free at:

If You Find a Rock

Description

Learners observe the phenomenon that there are many different kinds of rocks with different properties. They observe, describe, and sort a variety of rocks and are introduced to various ways that rocks form. Then they explore different uses of rocks based on their properties.

Alignment with the *Next Generation Science Standards*

Performance Expectations

2-ESS1-1: Use information from several sources to provide evidence that Earth events can occur quickly or slowly.

2-PS1-1: Analyze data obtained from testing different materials to determine which materials have the properties that are best suited for an intended purpose.

Science and Engineering Practices	Disciplinary Core Ideas	Crosscutting Concept
Analyzing and Interpreting Data Record information (observations, thoughts, and ideas.) Use and share pictures, drawings, and/or writings of observations. **Obtaining, Evaluating, and Communicating Information** Read grade-appropriate texts and/or use media to obtain scientific and/or technical information to determine patterns in and/or evidence about the natural and designed world(s). Obtain information using various texts, text features (e.g., headings, tables of contents, glossaries, electronic menus, icons), and other media that will be useful in answering a scientific question and/or supporting a scientific claim.	**ESS1.C: The History of Planet Earth** Some events happen very quickly; others occur very slowly over a period of time much longer than one can observe. **PS1.A: Structure and Properties of Matter** Different properties are suited to different purposes.	**Stability and Change** Things may change slowly or rapidly.

Note: The activities in this lesson will help students move toward the performance expectations listed, which is the goal after multiple activities. However, the activities will not by themselves be sufficient to reach the performance expectations.

Featured Picture Books

TITLE: *If You Find a Rock*
AUTHOR: **Peggy Christian**
PHOTOGRAPHER: **Barbara Hirsch Lember**
PUBLISHER: **Harcourt**
YEAR: **2000**
GENRE: **Story**
SUMMARY: *Soft, hand-tinted photographs and simple, poetic text celebrate the variety of rocks that can be found, including skipping rocks, chalk rocks, and splashing rocks.*

TITLE: *Rocks: Hard, Soft, Smooth, and Rough*
AUTHOR: **Natalie Myra Rosinky**
ILLUSTRATOR: **Matthew John**
PUBLISHER: **Picture Window Books**
YEAR: **2002**
GENRE: **Non-Narrative Information**
SUMMARY: *Simple text and cartoonish illustrations provide information on igneous, sedimentary, and metamorphic rocks.*

Time Needed

This lesson will take several class periods. Suggested scheduling is as follows:

Session 1: Engage with *If You Find a Rock* Read-Aloud

Session 2: Explore with I Found a Rock and Rock Sorting

Session 3: Explain with *Rocks: Hard, Soft, Smooth, and Rough* Read-Aloud and Volcano Video

Session 4: Elaborate with Comparing Rocks Venn Diagram and If Rocks Could Talk Interviews

Session 5: Evaluate with Pet Rock Posters

Materials

For I Found a Rock (per student)

- Rock (brought in by student)
- Hand lens
- Centimeter ruler

For Rocks: Hard, Soft, Smooth, and Rough *Read-Aloud*

- One of each of the following rock samples: obsidian, granite, sandstone, limestone, and marble (per group of 5 students)
- Hand lens (1 per student)

For Comparing Rocks Venn Diagram

- 1 obsidian and 1 granite rock (per group of 4–6 students)
- Hand lens (1 per student)

For If Rocks Could Talk Interviews

- Tape or glue

For Pet Rock Posters

- Colored pencils, crayons, or markers
- Poster board
- Highlighter
- Glue stick
- Optional: Photo of the original Pet Rock packaging

Rock specimens in packs of 10 are available from *www.carolina.com*

Rock	Order Number
Obsidian, Black	GEO1112B
Granite, Gray	GEO1080B
Sandstone, Red	GEO2012B
Limestone, Fossil	GEO1198B
Marble, White	GEO2054B

Student Pages

- I Found a Rock
- Comparing Rocks Venn Diagram
- If Rocks Could Talk
- Pet Rock Advertising Poster Rubric
- STEM Everywhere

Background for Teachers

Children are naturally curious about the world around them, including the rocks beneath their feet. Learning about the properties and uses of Earth's materials, such as rocks, helps young children build a foundation for understanding the interactions of Earth's *geosphere* (crust, mantle, and core), *hydrosphere* (water), *atmosphere* (air), and *biosphere* (living things). Earth materials have different physical and chemical properties that make them useful in different ways. This lesson focuses primarily on the phenomenon that there are many different kinds of rocks with different properties. Students learn how to identify and describe these properties (shape, size, color, texture, and luster—but not hardness, which is a property used to identify minerals only) and explore how properties of rocks, including the presence of crystals, can be used to sort them. They learn that the properties of color, texture, and luster are useful for identifying different rock types, but the properties of size and shape are not. They also explore how a rock's properties and its uses are related.

Through observation and reading, students learn that rocks can be classified as igneous, sedimentary, or metamorphic depending on how they are formed. *Igneous* rock occurs when hot, molten rock, or *magma*, cools and solidifies. Magma originates deep within Earth near active plate boundaries or hot spots, then rises toward the surface. Most magma remains trapped underground and cools very slowly over many thousands or millions of years until it solidifies. This process forms *intrusive* igneous rock. These rocks typically cool so slowly that they have time to develop large crystals. Examples of intrusive igneous rock include *granite* and *gabbro*. Extrusive igneous rock is formed when magma exits Earth's

surface through cracks or erupting volcanoes. Magma, called lava when it reaches the surface, cools and solidifies very quickly when it is exposed to water or to the atmosphere. Mineral crystals don't have much time to grow, so extrusive igneous rocks, such as *basalt*, have a very fine-grained texture. *Obsidian* is a volcanic glass that forms when a particular type of lava cools almost instantly.

Rocks can also form when *sediments*, such as sand, mud, pebbles, bones, shells, and plants, settle into layers on the bottoms of lakes, oceans, or rivers. Over millions of years, the top layers press down on the bottom layers and the bottom layers become *sedimentary* rock. *Sandstone* and *limestone* are examples of sedimentary rock. Limestone often contains the fossilized remains of animals that lived millions of years ago.

The third type of rock is *metamorphic* rock—rock that was formed when another kind of rock was exposed to tremendous heat and pressure over a long period of time. For example, *marble* is a metamorphic rock formed when limestone is "squeezed and cooked" inside Earth. The minerals within metamorphic rock are often arranged in stripes or swirls caused by heat and uneven pressure.

Although the rock cycle is not a focus of this lesson, students learn that rocks can melt inside Earth. They also read about some of the other processes that can create and transform the types of rocks in Earth's crust. Students are introduced to the concept of fast and slow changes to Earth's surface by learning about volcanoes and comparing how different igneous rocks are formed. Some volcanic igneous rocks can form very quickly but most types of rock are formed over thousands or millions of years. Students will build on these concepts in later grades when they learn how patterns of rock formations can reveal changes over time and how the presence and location of certain fossil types indicate the order in which rock layers were formed.

In this lesson, students apply the science and engineering practice (SEP) of analyzing and interpreting data as they record and share their observations of different types of rocks. They use the SEP of obtaining, evaluating, and communicating information as they read about different types of rocks and how they are formed, as well as the properties of rocks and their uses. Students apply the crosscutting concept (CCC) of stability and change as they discuss how some events on Earth, such as volcanic eruptions, happen very quickly, whereas others occur over a time period much longer than one can observe.

Learning Progressions

Below are the disciplinary core idea (DCI) grade band endpoints for grades K–2 and 3–5. These are provided to show how student understanding of the DCIs in this lesson will progress in future grade levels.

DCIs	Grades K–2	Grades 3–5
ESS1.C: The History of Planet Earth	• Some events happen very quickly; others occur very slowly; over a time period much longer than one can observe.	• Local, regional, and global patterns of rock formations reveal changes over time due to Earth forces such as earthquakes. The presence and location of certain fossil types indicate the order in which rock layers were formed.
PS1.A: Structure and Properties of Matter	• Different properties are suited to different purposes.	• Measurements of a variety of properties can be used to identify materials..

Source: Willard, T., ed. 2015. *The NSTA quick-reference guide to the* NGSS: *Elementary school.* Arlington, VA: NSTA Press.

engage

If You Find a Rock Read-Aloud

Hold a piece of obsidian and a piece of granite behind your back. Then announce to the class that you have found some things that are older than them, older than the school building, even older than you … things that could even be millions of years old! Have students guess what they are. Reveal the rocks, and then tell students that rocks are probably the oldest things that they will ever touch. Pass around the rocks, and ask students to share observations. *Ask*

? How can you describe the rocks?

? How are they alike? How are they different?

? Do you think they are the same kind of rock?

? How do you think the rocks formed?

? How long do you think it takes rocks to form?

? What could these rocks be used for?

? What other questions do you have about the rocks?

Then tell students that you have a book to read to get them thinking about rocks.

Making Connections: Text to Self

Introduce the author and photographer of the book *If You Find a Rock*. The author, Peggy Christian, is a rock hound who was born in the Rocky Mountains of Colorado and loves skiing, camping, and reading. Build connections to the author by *asking*

? What is a *rock hound*? (a person who likes to collect rocks)

? Is anyone here a rock hound? (Answers will vary.)

? What do you call a scientist who studies rocks to learn about Earth? (a geologist)

? Would you like to be a geologist? (Answers will vary.)

Explain that there are many people, both men and women, who choose geology as a career and devote their entire lives to studying it. Tell students that Peggy Christian's father was a geologist and maybe that is why she loves rocks so much.

Determining Importance

Explain that, while you are reading the book aloud, you would like students to think about what some of the rocks in the book are used for and what properties, or characteristics, make them suited for those uses.

Read aloud *If You Find a Rock*. (For fun, stop after reading the page about the wishing rock and invite students to close their eyes and make a wish.)

IF YOU FIND A ROCK *READ-ALOUD*

After reading, *ask*

? What are some of the uses for the special rocks in the book? (Answers might include wishing rock, skipping rock, chalk rock, resting rock, splashing rock, and worry rock.)

? Have you ever owned a special rock?

? What made it special to you?

Tell students that they are going to be rock hounds on the hunt for their own special rock. They can select a rock from their own collection or, with adult supervision, find one outside. They should bring their special rock to school the next day. Send a letter home to inform parents of the assignment. Include these rules for students to follow: *Your rock must be smaller than a tennis ball. You are not allowed to throw your rock.* You may want to have extra rocks available for students who don't bring one in.

explore

I Found a Rock

The next day, have students place their rocks on their tables or desks. Ask them to observe their own rock and then look around at some of the rocks near them. Discuss the following questions:

? How are the rocks alike?

? How are the rocks different?

Encourage students to notice that rocks come in a wide variety of colors, shapes, sizes, and other characteristics. Then explain that a scientific tool called a hand lens can help them get an even closer look at their rocks. Demonstrate the proper way to use a hand lens (holding the lens close to one eye while bringing the rock toward the hand lens until it comes into focus), and caution them that touching the rock to the surface of the hand lens can scratch the lens. Pass out hand lenses to all students, and have them use the lenses to observe their rock more closely.

Next, revisit the book *If You Find a Rock*. Ask students to recall the rocks described in the book. List some of the rocks on the board, such as:

- skipping rock
- chalk rock
- resting rock

- wishing rock
- worry rock
- climbing rock

Then *ask*

? What makes each rock in the book suited for its special use? (Answers might include its shape, its color or size, and how it feels.)

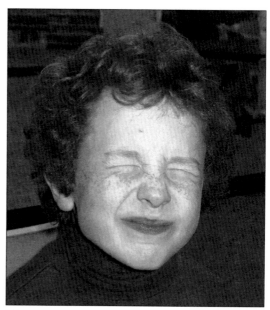

MAKING A WISH

Explain that these things—shape, color, size, texture (how it feels)—are called *properties* of rocks. Discuss how the properties of each rock in the book make it suited for a different purpose. For example, a skipping rock is used for skipping across water. The properties that make it suited for that purpose are its flat, rounded *shape* and its small *size*. Shape and size are properties of rocks. A chalk rock is used to draw pictures on pavement. The properties that make it suited for that purpose are its white *color* and its soft, dusty *texture*. Color and texture are also properties of rocks. Another property students may notice as they observe their rocks is *luster*, or how the rocks reflect light. Words that describe luster include *shiny, dull,* and *sparkly*.

Explain that shape, size, color, texture, and luster are different properties of rocks that make each one unique. Geologists who study rocks use some of these properties to identify different types of rocks. Tell students that they are going to observe and record the properties of their own special rock.

Connecting to the Common Core
Mathematics
MEASUREMENT AND DATA: 2.MD.A.1

Pass out the I Found a Rock student page and centimeter rulers. Make sure students understand how to record the properties listed on the data table (color, texture, luster, size) by *asking*

? What are some words that might describe a rock's *color*? (Answers might include *black*, *white*, and *reddish-brown*.)

? What are some words that might describe a rock's *texture*? (Answers might include *bumpy*, *smooth*, and *rough*.)

? What are some words that might describe a rock's *luster*? (Answers might include *shiny*, *dull*, and *glassy*.)

? What is one way to measure a rock's *size*? (Use a ruler to measure the longest side in centimeters.)

> **SEP: Analyzing and Interpreting Data**
> Record information (observations, thoughts, and ideas.)Use and share pictures, drawings, and/or writings of observations.

Discuss how observations of size, such as big or small, are not scientific observations because they are not exact. Using measurements to describe the size of a rock is more scientific. Then have students

MEASURING A ROCK

make careful observations of their rocks and complete their data tables.

Next, have students think about the unique properties of their rocks and fill in this cloze sentence: "I found a rock that would be good for _____ because it is _____."

Rock Sorting

This activity is a fun way to show that rocks can be identified by their unique properties. The object is to end with one student standing, holding his or her rock. Collect all of the I Found a Rock student pages. Randomly select one from the stack, but don't let students see it. Have all the students stand, holding their rocks. Then read the first observation on the page, for example, "I found a rock, and it is gray. If your rock is gray, stay standing." Students whose rocks are not gray should sit. Then read the second observation on the page, for example, "I found a rock, and it is smooth. If your rock is smooth, stay standing." Students whose rocks are not smooth should sit. Continue reading the obser-

vations, including the cloze sentence at the bottom, until only one student is standing. Repeat the process with several more student pages. Then *ask*

? What have you learned about rocks? (Students should recognize that rocks have different properties.)

? What are you still wondering about rocks? (Answers will vary.)

explain

Rocks: Hard, Soft, Smooth, and Rough Read-Aloud and Volcano Video

Connecting to the Common Core
Reading: Informational Text
KEY IDEAS AND DETAILS: 2.3

USING THE ROCK IDENTIFICATION CHART

Form groups of five students. Give each student a hand lens and one of the following rocks: obsidian, granite, sandstone, limestone, or marble. Have each student observe his or her rock and compare it to the other rocks in their group. *Ask*

? Are the five rocks all the same kind of rock? (no)

? How are they different? (They have different properties: shape, size, color, texture, and luster.)

? Is it possible to look at a rock and tell what kind of rock it is? (Answers will vary. The following activity will help students understand how geologists identify rocks by their properties.)

> **SEP: Obtaining, Evaluating, and Communicating Information**
> Read grade-appropriate texts to obtain scientific information to determine patterns in and/or evidence about the natural world. Obtain information using various texts, text features (e.g. headings, tables of contents, glossaries, electronic menus, icons that will be useful in supporting a scientific claim.

Next, tell students that the picture book *Rocks: Hard, Soft, Smooth, and Rough* can give them clues about their rock's identity. Each one of the rocks they have been observing is described in the book. Read the book aloud, being sure to read the "fun facts" that are inset on some of the pages. Pause after reading each rock description and ask students to hold up their rock if they think it is the one being described.

After reading, use the rocks chart on page 21 to help students identify their rocks correctly. Explain that many different kinds of scientists use these kinds of charts, also called keys, to identify

unknown objects. After reading, use the following questions to help students understand how size and shape might not be good properties to use to identify rocks. *Ask*

? What properties did you use to identify your rock? (Answers might include color, texture, luster, swirls, stripes, or specks.)

? Were you able to identify your rock based on its size or shape alone? (no)

? Is size a good property to use to identify a type of rock? Why or why not? (No, because rocks are all different sizes depending on how they formed or broke apart from larger rocks.)

? Is shape a good property to use to identify a type of rock? (No, for the same reason as in the previous question.)

? What are the basic building blocks of rocks called? (minerals)

Next, have students use hand lenses to see if they can find any swirls, stripes, or shiny specks called crystals in their rock samples. These features are made by the minerals that make up their rocks. Some rocks are made of a single mineral, but most are made of several minerals. (A student who is observing a very fine-grained rock may not be able to see any minerals. Geologists often use special microscopes to look at very thin slices of rocks so they can determine mineral content and thus rock type.) Then *ask*

? How do scientists identify unknown rocks? (They can observe their properties and use a key.)

? What are the three main types of rocks you learned about in the book? (igneous, sedimentary, and metamorphic)

? How are rocks classified into these three groups? (Rocks are classified based on how they are formed.)

Making Connections: Text-to-Text

Revisit page 10 of *Rocks: Hard, Soft, Smooth, and Rough*. Point to the picture of the volcano and *ask*

? Does anyone know what this is called? (a volcano)

? What is the melted rock that comes out of a volcano called? (Answers will vary.)

Explain that when melted rock comes to Earth's surface it is called lava, but when it is *underground*, it is called magma. Point out the pool of magma below the picture of the volcano on page 10. Then *ask*

? Have you ever seen a volcano erupting?

? Would you like to see a video of a real volcanic eruption?

Show students the video titled "Iceland Volcano: Drone footage captures stunning up-close view of eruption" (see "Websites") or another video of an erupting volcano. Tell students that there are more than 1,500 active volcanoes on Earth and that this one is located in Iceland. Point out Iceland on a map. After watching the video, *ask*

? How do you think this video was taken? (by a drone, an aircraft without a human pilot)

? Why do you think a drone was used? (It would not be safe for a person to be that close to an erupting volcano.)

? What did you notice? (Answers will vary, but students may notice that lava is shooting from the volcano and pouring down the sides. They may also notice that the sides and base of the volcano are made of black rock.)

? What do you wonder? (Answers will vary.)

? Where do you think all the black rock on the volcano came from? (It came from the hot lava that cooled and turned into rock.)

Explain that an erupting volcano is an example of rock forming quickly. The hot lava is liquid

rock that can instantly turn into solid rock when it hits the air. *Ask*

? Does all rock form this quickly? (no)

> **CCC: Stability and Changee**
> Things may change slowly or rapidly.

Students may remember from the book, *Rocks: Hard, Soft, Smooth, and Rough* that some rocks take a long time to form. Revisit the following pages that share these examples:

- Page 13 says that sedimentary rock can take millions of years to form.
- Page 17 says that fossils are made from plants and animals that died thousands or millions of years ago. Over time, they turned into rock.
- Page 18 says that over time, heat and pressure can turn a metamorphic rock into a new metamorphic rock.

Explain that some rocks form quickly and others form very slowly, over a period of time longer than one can observe. Tell students that in the next activity, they will be comparing two different kinds of rocks in order to learn more about how some rocks form quickly and others form slowly.

elaborate

Comparing Rocks Venn Diagram

*Venn Diagram*

Show students the two rocks you shared in the engage phase of the lesson—obsidian and granite. Give each group of 4–6 students a sample of each and the Comparing Rocks Venn Diagram student page. Tell students that one tool they can use to compare how things are alike and different is a Venn diagram. Have students observe the two rocks again with hand lenses. Then cut out each statement at the bottom of the student page and

COMPARING ROCKS

work with a partner to place the statements in the Venn diagram. Explain that if they are not sure at this point, that is OK. They will have a chance to resort the statements after doing some reading.

After students have had a chance to cut and sort the statements, *ask*

? If these rocks could talk, what do you think they could tell you? (Answers will vary.)

Tell students that every rock has a "story" to tell—its age, where it formed, how it formed, what it is made of, what it could be used for, etc. Geologists observe and test rocks to figure out their "stories." *Ask*

? Wouldn't it be fun to interview a rock to find out its story?

If Rocks Could Talk Interviews

1. Divide the class into groups of 4–6 students.
2. Give each student a copy of the If Rocks Could Talk student page. Have them quickly scan the text and notice the text features.
3. Ask, "What do you notice about the text?"

(It is about rocks, the rocks can talk, it is written as a script/interview/reader's theater/play, it is mostly dialogue, it has a cast of characters, there are different characters or roles, it is divided into two parts or episodes, etc.)

4. Ask, "Who are the different characters in the cast?" (Announcer, Geologist, Obsidian, Quartz)

5. Explain that each student in a group will have a speaking part. If there are four students in their group, each student will be either the Announcer, the Geologist, Obsidian, or Quartz. If there are five students, they will have a different Geologist for each episode. If there are six students, they will have a different Geologist and a different Announcer for each episode.

6. Have the students in each group divide up the speaking parts, or assign them yourself. (Note that the Announcer has the fewest lines.)

7. Ask students to read the script silently, paying close attention to any information that can help them complete their Venn diagrams.

8. Have students highlight and practice their own speaking part.

9. Have students perform the script within their own groups.

10. Optional: Choose a group or invite a group to volunteer, and have the students perform a reader's theater for the whole class. A reader's theater is a style of theater in which the actors read aloud from a script without costumes, scenery, or much movement. Actors rely on vocal expression to tell the story.

> **CCC: Stability and Change**
> Things may change slowly or rapidly.

After the If Rocks Could Talk activity, have students return to their Venn diagrams and work with their group or a partner to check their answers using information from the scripts. They may need to move the statements to the correct place. After they complete the Venn diagram, have them tape or glue the statements onto the paper. Answers are as follows:

Obsidian	Both	Granite
smooth texture	Formed from melted rock	rough texture
Cooled quickly from lava above ground		Cooled slowly from magma underground
Used for knives and arrowheads	Has many uses	Used for gravestones and countertops

If Rocks Could Talk Reader's Theater

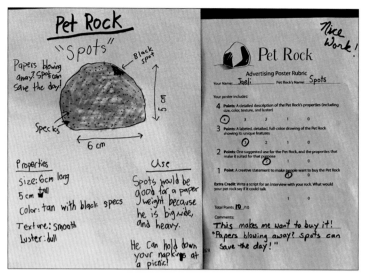

PET ROCK ADVERTISEMENT

evaluate

Pet Rock Posters

> **Connecting to the Common Core**
> **Writing**
> TEXT TYPES AND PURPOSES: 2.2

Ask students if they have ever heard of a Pet Rock. Explain that way back in 1975, a businessman in California came up with the idea of selling rocks as pets. He considered dogs, cats, and birds too messy and expensive to keep and instead advertised his Pet Rock as the ideal pet. The Pet Rock was packaged in a box that looked like a pet carrying case, and it even came with a "Pet Rock Training Manual." Topics included "How to Make Your Pet Rock Roll Over and Play Dead" and "How to House-Train Your Pet Rock." Believe it or not, the Pet Rock became a huge hit and the salesman became rich. (Optional: Show students a photo of the original Pet Rock and its packaging.) *Ask*

? Would you have bought your own Pet Rock if you lived in the 1970s?

? Why do you think this businessman was able to sell so many Pet Rocks? (Answers might include: He had an original idea, and he used creative packaging and advertising.)

? What are some ways that advertisements help sell products? (Answers might include: They describe them, they make them sound useful, and they make them seem fun.)

Pass out the Pet Rock Poster Rubric student page and challenge students to create an advertisement for a Pet Rock. You may want to have them use either their own special rock or the rock they identified using the book *Rocks: Hard, Soft, Smooth, and Rough*. Have them give their rock a clever name ("Dusty," "Rocky," and "Cliff" come to mind!) and then design an ad to sell the rock. The advertisement should show what they have learned about properties of rocks, including:

- **4 Points:** A detailed description of the Pet Rock's properties (including size, color, texture, and luster)
- **3 Points:** A labeled, detailed, full-color drawing of the Pet Rock showing its unique features
- **2 Points:** One suggested use for the Pet Rock and the properties that make it suited for that purpose
- **1 Point:** A creative statement to make people want to buy the Pet Rock
- **Extra Credit:** Write a script for an interview with your rock. What would your Pet Rock say if it could talk?

Have students share their advertisements with the rest of the class or have a gallery walk.

STEM Everywhere

Give students the STEM Everywhere student page as a way to involve their families and extend their learning. They can do the activity with an adult helper and share their results with the class. If students do not have the internet at home, you may choose to have them complete this activity at school.

National Science Teaching Association

Opportunities for Differentiated Instruction

This box lists questions and challenges related to the lesson that students may select to research, investigate, or innovate. Students may also use the questions as examples to help them generate their own questions. These questions can help you move your students from the teacher-directed investigation to engaging in the science and engineering practices in a more student-directed format.

Extra Support

For students who are struggling to meet the lesson objectives, provide a question and guide them in the process of collecting research or helping them design procedures or solutions.

Extensions

For students with high interest or who have already met the lesson objectives, have them choose a question (or pose their own question), conduct their own research, and design their own procedures or solutions.

After selecting one of the questions in the box or formulating their own question, students can individually or collaboratively make predictions, design investigations or surveys to test their predictions, collect evidence, devise explanations, design solutions, or examine related resources. They can communicate their findings through a science notebook, at a poster session or gallery walk, or by producing a media project.

Research

Have students brainstorm researchable questions:

? What are some common rocks that can be found in your state? What are they used for?

? What are some different kinds of geologists? What do they do?

? What technologies help geologists explore volcanoes?

Investigate

Have students brainstorm testable questions to be solved through science or math:

? Can you use Moh's Hardness Scale to test different minerals for hardness? (See *Rocks: Hard, Soft, Smooth, and Rough* page 23)

? How can you measure the volume of a rock (how much space it takes up)?

? Can you make your own sandstone brick? (See *Rocks: Hard, Soft, Smooth, and Rough* page 22)

Innovate

Have students brainstorm problems to be solved through engineering:

? Can you design a display case for a rock collection?

? Can you design and create a mosaic, balanced rock sculpture, birdhouse, etc. using small rocks?

? Can you design a robot that could explore an active volcano? Draw it!

Websites

 "Iceland volcano: Drone footage captures stunning up-close view of eruption" (video)
www.youtube.com/watch?v=b9Hq6bTBF2A

 If Rocks Could Talk (interviews adapted from American Museum of Natural History Website)
www.amnh.org/explore/ology/earth/if-rocks-could-talk2/obsidian

More Books to Read

Baylor, B. 1985. *Everybody needs a rock*. New York: Aladdin.

Summary: Everybody needs a rock—at least that's the way this particular rock hound feels about it in presenting her own highly individualistic rules for finding just the right rock for you.

Hooper, M. 2015. *The pebble in my pocket: A history of our Earth*. New York: Viking Juvenile.

Summary: A girl finds a pebble on the ground and wonders where it came from. The answer unfolds through scientifically accurate text, colorful illustrations, and a helpful timeline that follows the pebble's long journey from the inside of a volcano to the day the girl picks it up off the ground.

Miller, P. 2021. *What can you do with a rock?* Naperville, IL: Sourcebooks.

Summary: Simple text and colorful illustrations answer the question, what can you do with a rock?

Salas, L. 2015. *A rock can be…* Minneapolis: Millbrook Press.

Summary: From Salas and Dabija, the team who created *A Leaf Can Be…* and *Water Can Be…*, this book sparks the reader's imagination by sharing some of the many things a rock can be: a tall mountain, a park fountain, a food grinder, a path winder, and so on.

Wenzel, B. 2019. *A stone sat still*. San Francisco: Chronicle Books.

Summary: This beautifully illustrated book tells the story of a stone that seems ordinary. But to the animals that encounter the stone, it serves many purposes.

National Science Teaching Association

I Found a Rock

Color What colors or patterns does it have?	Texture How does it feel?	Luster How shiny or dull is it?	Size What is the longest length in cm?

Labeled Drawing of My Rock

I found a rock that would be good for _____

because it is _____ .

Comparing Rocks Venn Diagram

Directions: Observe the two rocks with a hand lens. Then cut out the statements at the bottom of the page, and place each statement below Obsidian, Granite, or Both.

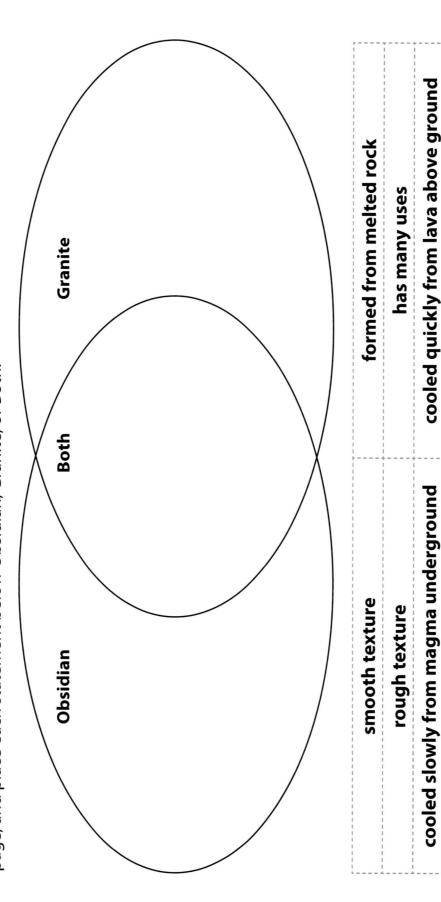

Granite

Both

Obsidian

formed from melted rock

has many uses

cooled quickly from lava above ground

used for knives and arrowheads

smooth texture

rough texture

cooled slowly from magma underground

used for gravestones and countertops

16

Name: _____

If Rocks Could Talk

Episode 1

Cast: Announcer, Geologist, Obsidian

ANNOUNCER: Welcome to the show "If Rocks Could Talk!"

ALL: (*clapping*)

ANNOUNCER: Can rocks talk? Of course not! But if they could, we're here to find out what they would say.

GEOLOGIST: My name is Dr. _____. I'm a geologist.

ANNOUNCER: A geologist is a scientist who studies the Earth's surface.

GEOLOGIST: Indeed. I'll be your geologist on this episode of "If Rocks Could Talk." Today we're going to meet a rock with a very interesting story.

OBSIDIAN: Can we get started already? I don't have all day!

GEOLOGIST: Sorry folks, Obsidian is a bit hot-tempered. I guess that's what happens when you erupt from a volcano.

OBSIDIAN: Very funny.

GEOLOGIST: So, tell us how you formed.

OBSIDIAN: Well, it all began deep underground. There's so much heat and pressure down there that rocks can melt!

ANNOUNCER: You heard it here first, folks. Rocks can melt!

OBSIDIAN: They sure can. Did you know there are pools of hot melted rock called magma miles below the Earth's surface?

GEOLOGIST: I knew that. But go on.

OBSIDIAN: And if there's a crack or weak zone above it, that magma is gonna blow!

GEOLOGIST: Indeed it is.

OBSIDIAN: Next thing you know, you've got yourself a volcanic eruption!

If Rocks Could Talk, Episode 1, Continued

GEOLOGIST: What happens then?

OBSIDIAN: Well, when the magma reaches the surface, it's called lava. The lava flows out and cools off. I formed above ground when some of that lava cooled.

GEOLOGIST: Well, I "lava" your smooth texture.

ANNOUNCER: Let's take a short break to observe Obsidian's texture! (*Everyone looks at obsidian using hand lenses.*)

ALL (*Except Obsidian*): Ooohhh, pretty!

OBSIDIAN: Pretty sharp, too. In fact, Native Americans used to carve obsidian into knives and arrowheads.

GEOLOGIST: Why are you so smooth and sharp? I don't see any crystals at all!

OBSIDIAN: I don't know if you've ever seen a volcano erupt –

GEOLOGIST: No, but it would really "mag-ma" day!

OBSIDIAN: Very funny. Anyway, some events on Earth, like volcanic eruptions, happen very quickly. And hot lava can cool off quickly when it hits air or water.

GEOLOGIST: And?

OBSIDIAN: When a certain type of lava cools very quickly, obsidian can form!

GEOLOGIST: And?

OBSIDIAN: When you cool and harden that fast, you don't have time to form big, shiny crystals like some rocks. You're just...glass. (*looks sad*)

GEOLOGIST: Don't be sad! Your properties may be different, but they make you special. I mean, not all rocks can be used for arrowheads!

ANNOUNCER: And there you have it, folks! Rocks have different properties!

ALL: (*clapping*)

Adapted from www.amnh.org/explore/ology/earth/if-rocks-could-talk2

National Science Teaching Association

If Rocks Could Talk

Episode 2

Cast: Announcer, Geologist, Granite

ANNOUNCER: Welcome to the second episode of "If Rocks Could Talk!"

ALL: (*clapping*)

GEOLOGIST: My name is Dr. _____. I'm a geologist. On our last episode, we spoke with Obsidian. Obsidian is a smooth, shiny volcanic rock that can form when lava cools very quickly above ground. Our next guest will answer the question "What happens when magma cools very slowly underground?" (*looks around for Granite*)

GRANITE: Yo. I'm right here.

GEOLOGIST: Oh, sorry, Granite, I didn't see you there. You're not quite as flashy as Obsidian.

GRANITE: I may not be flashy, but don't just take me for "granite."

GEOLOGIST: You're a real joker, aren't you?

GRANITE: Yeah, I had like, thousands of years to think of jokes while I was cooling off.

GEOLOGIST: Thousands of years indeed. Anyway, on our last episode, we learned that some changes on Earth happen very quickly. Volcanic eruptions. The cooling of lava into obsidian. But other events happen very slowly, over a period of time much longer than any human can observe. The formation of the Grand Canyon. The cooling of magma into —

GRANITE: Yo, you want me to tell my story or what?

GEOLOGIST: Oh, so you're a tough guy.

GRANITE: You could say that. I mean, haven't you ever seen gravestones made of granite? Countertops? Buildings? You ever been to Mount Rushmore?

If Rocks Could Talk, Episode 2, Continued

GEOLOGIST: OK, I get it, you're strong.

GRANITE: I sure am. So here's my story. A few billion years ago, I formed from melted rock.

GEOLOGIST: Like Obsidian did.

GRANITE: Yeah, but not quite like that. I didn't shoot out of a volcano like Obsidian. I took my time, kept it on the "down low."

GEOLOGIST: Are you saying you formed in a pocket of hot, liquid magma deep underground?

GRANITE: Yeah, sure. Took thousands of years for that magma to cool down. In fact, I cooled so slowly I had plenty of time to grow all these shiny specks.

GEOLOGIST: Crystals? Mind if we take a closer look?

ANNOUNCER: Let's take a short break to look at Granite's crystals! (*Everyone looks at Granite using hand lenses.*)

ALL (*Except Granite*): Ooohhh, pretty crystals!

GRANITE: Aw, shucks!

GEOLOGIST: You know, Granite, even though you have a rough texture, you are pretty cool.

GRANITE: Yeah, well, sorry we got off to a rocky start.

GEOLOGIST: No hard feelings.

ANNOUNCER: And there you have it, folks! Rocks can form quickly or rocks can form slowly. Rocks have different properties. Annnnd...rocks can be very useful!

ALL: (*clapping*)

GRANITE: Rocks rock!

GEOLOGIST: Indeed!

Adapted from www.amnh.org/explore/ology/earth/if-rocks-could-talk2

National Science Teaching Association

Pet Rock

Advertising Poster Rubric

Your Name: _____ Pet Rock's Name: _____

Your poster includes:

4 **Points**: A detailed description of the Pet Rock's properties (including size, color, texture, and luster)

    4   3   2   1   0

3 **Points**: A labeled, detailed, full-color drawing of the Pet Rock showing its unique features

        3   2   1   0

2 **Points**: One suggested use for the Pet Rock and the properties that make it suited for that purpose

            2   1   0

1 **Point**: A creative statement to make people want to buy the Pet Rock

                1   0

Extra Credit: Write a script for an interview with your rock. What would your pet rock say if it could talk?

                1   0

Total Points_____/10

Comments:

_____

_____

Name: _____

STEM Everywhere

Dear Families,

At school, we have been learning about rocks. We learned that rocks have different properties and can be used for different purposes. We also learned that some rocks form quickly and others form slowly. To find out more, ask your learner the following questions and discuss their answers:

- What did you learn?
- What was your favorite part of the lesson?
- What are you still wondering?

You can watch a video together called "Scientist Profile: Rock Scientist," which features a geologist working in the field and lab.

 To watch the video, scan the QR code, go to *www.pbslearningmedia. org* and search for "Rock Scientist," or go to *www.pbslearningmedia. org/resource/46106c1c-0ed0-4887-af0e-fcc523739dfd/46106c1c-0ed0-4887-af0e-fcc523739dfd*

After you watch the video, look around your neighborhood and notice rocks being used for different purposes (building materials, decorations, landscaping, etc.). Draw or write the ways you see rocks being used below.

National Science Teaching Association